FRO GURL CHRONICLES

BOOK TWO

Poems by Erica Dubois

Soft Power. Sharp Tongue.

Unapologetically Grown.

For every woman.

Mom, I miss your voice...

WRITE IT, SIS

This space is for your truth. Your voice. Your fire.

Let it out--uncensored, unedited, unapologetic.

Contents

His Lips Smelled Like Double-mint Gum & Cigarettes ... 9

Sis, I Ain't Sorry ... 11

He Was Fine But Exhausting ... 12

The Side Eye ... 13

I Protest, I Sit, I Wait... and the Same Shit ... 14

Voodoo Queen ... 15

People Stop Saying Thank You ... 16

No Ring? He's Married ... 17

If I Should Die Before I Drink ... 18

How Many Ways to Say Fuck Off ... 19

How to Say Fuck Off at Work ... 20

Instant Gratification ... 21

My Afro, My Rules ... 22

We Detangle, But We Don't Explain ... 23

He Loved Me Out Loud ... 24

We Had Great Chemistry, Bad Timing, and No Business ... 25

What I Learned from a Broken Heart ... 27

Looking for a New Kind of Love ... 28

Traveled Across the World, Only to Come Back to This ... 30

Cakes, Pies, Cookies, and Weed ... 31

My Next Gig Will Be for Me ... 32

My Makeup Brushes Tell a Story ... 33

That Fur Coat with Nothing Underneath ... 34

Lipstick, Wine, and Late-Night Danger ... 35

I Overheard Your Ignorance and I Love It..37
Money Money No Money..39
A Hustler's Fatigue..40
The Side-By Affair..41
I've Become Emotionally Unavailable..43
Lemon Drop Martinis and Truffle Fries...44
Slipping Into My Darkness..45
He Kissed My Toes Like A Pro...46
Air Kiss Me in the Dark..47
I Don't Chase Ghosts, I Name Them..48
His Energy...49
Strength Comes in Numbers...50
My Sisterhood Is for My Sister Hood..51
Sometimes I Smell Like a French Whore, and I Loved It..........53
His Strut Got Me Trippin'...55

His Lips Smelled Like Double-mint Gum & Cigarettes

His lips?

Minty lies wrapped in smoke.

Double-mint gum and cigarettes— Sweet at first, then bitter if you breathe too deep.

He said my name

like a match strike, like I was the flame he promised he'd stop playing with.

We kissed in the hush between streetlights, lip gloss clinging to his breath, his cool pretending to cover something burning.

He said he quit.

I nodded.

Didn't ask what.

Didn't believe it either.

Sometimes,

I still taste the spark, that perfect blend of temptation and trash.

And if I’m honest?

Some nights,

I want it back.

Sis, I Ain't Sorry

I left the party early,
Took my peace and my purse.
Didn't offer no long explanation— Didn't feel like being rehearsed.

I don't dim no more,
Don't shrink to fit the frame.
I sip slow, I walk bold,
And I answer to my name.

I ain't sorry for the no-call,
Or the "I'll see you when I see you."
Sis, I've spent too many years
Trying to be what will not free you.

He Was Fine But Exhausting

He had cheekbones carved by chaos, A smile that knew it. A voice deep like Sunday morning, But baby, I been through it.

He walked in like jazz— All smooth, all swing.

But he left like a voicemail

That didn't say a damn thing.

We had coffee, we had chemistry, He had theories, I had time.

But his energy needed managing— And I wasn't about to give him mine

See, I don't chase pretty no more.

I watch it, I sip it, I nod.

But if your soul is on E

But your face praises God...

I'm good, love.

Fine can't feed me.

You were art.

But I need energy.

The Side Eye

I didn't say a word— but my brow did.

My lashes tilted like,

"Who raised this kid?"

You kept talking.

And I kept sipping. My patience was doing a quiet backflipping.

I smiled.

But it was lowercase. The kind you give when someone's outta place.

You thought you were charming— bless your lil plan.

But my side eye was screaming:

"Ain't no grown woman buying that, man."

I've mastered the art of speaking through stares, Of giving a sermon without leaving my chair.

So tread lightly, and read the signs.

'Cause Fro Gurl don't bark— She just blinks... three times.

I Protest, I Sit, I Wait... and the Same Shit

I wore the shirt.

I marched the block.

I lit the candle.

I watched the clock.

Said the names.

Shared the thread.

Laid the flowers.

Counted the dead.

I voted.

I wept.

I prayed.

I pled.

And still... they shoot, they lie, we bled.

I protest,

I sit,

I waited...

And still the same shit

Voodoo Queen

They call me a witch, but I call it wisdom. My roots run deeper than your freedom system.

I wear gold and bone, oil and flame. I don't hex for sport— I call truth by name.

My altar ain't for play.

My prayers don't miss. I stir my tea with thunder and seal it with a kiss.

You scared 'cause I see you, naked in the mask. But don't worry, baby— I only hex when asked.

People Stop Saying Thank You

They stop saying thank you once they get used to your doing. Used to your showing up, your picking up, your knowing without asking.

They clap when you arrive.

But not when you stay.

Not when you carry.

Not when you bend.

They forget how heavy it was until you drop it. And suddenly, you're "acting different." You're "so ungrateful."

You "used to be so sweet."

Nah.

I used to be tired.

I used to be quiet.

I used to be thankless.

Now I say thank you to myself.

Out loud.

No Ring? He's Married

He said he was "free."

I said, "from what?" 'Cause freedom don't fidget when your phone lights up.

No ring on his hand—

but baby, I read energy. And he came with a silence too practiced for honesty.

He called me "queen." I called him a Lyft.

'Cause I don't date men still playing pretend with that shit

If you gotta explain her, you're still in it.

If you flinch when I grab your phone, you ain't finished.

No ring? He's married.

To the lie. To the thrill. To the comfort of a home he swears he's gonna rebuild.

And me?

I don't do demolition sites. I bless, I bounce, and I keep my spirit right

If I Should Die Before I Drink

If I should die before I drink, don't cry—just pour it in the sink. Let the bottle weep for me, the one I saved for company.

I bought that wine for a moment grand— a loud laugh a dancing hand.

But life kept saying, "Not just yet," and I kept saving with regret.

If I should die before the sip, take the glass—don't let it slip.

Raise it high, and tell the room:

She had joy she never used.

So drink your joy.

Don't wait like me.

Pour now, Drink the drink wild and free.

How Many Ways to Say Fuck Off

I could say: “I’m good, love.” Or:

“Bless your heart.” I could smile real slow, then just not take part.

I could ghost with grace.

I could block with style.

I could hit you with “I’ll think about it…” and never dial.

I could say: “That’s not aligned.” Or:

“I’m setting new intentions.” Or just stare and let the silence handle all the tension.

Because sometimes fuck off ain’t loud.

It’s soft.

It’s quiet.

It’s no. With no explanation behind it.

How to Say Fuck Off at Work

"I'll circle back."

(never will.)

"Let me check my bandwidth."

(it's full—with peace and snacks.)

"Per my last email..."

(That you clearly ignored, Chad.)

"I'm happy to help—after lunch."

(Translation: never.)

"That's above my pay grade."

(And I like it that way.)

"I'd love to, but I'm prioritizing self-preservation." Say it slow. Watch them blink.

Because sometimes

Fuck off at work sounds like "Let me know if you need anything else..." while you're already out the door.

Instant Gratification

I bought the dress.
Didn't wait for the sale.
Ate dessert first.
Skipped the email trail.

I texted back fast.
Laughed too loud.
Booked the trip.
Didn't ask the crowd.

Call it reckless.
Call it grown.
I just know what hits right to the bone.

I've waited before.
Saved. Delayed. But some joy don't like to be made.

It wants to be taken.
Right now.
Right here.
No guilt.
No pause.
Just—cheers.

My Afro, My Rules

Don't touch it.

Don't ask. Don't call it "wild." It ain't a task.

It's a crown, not a conversation.

Not a costume. Not a trend. It's the anthem I wear daily— A beginning and an end.

She leans toward the sun.

She moves how she please.

She don't shrink in the rain.

She don't beg to appease.

Edges laid or left alone, picked out high or hugged in tight— however, she shows up, she got that right.

My Afro,

My rules.

No debates.

Just roots.

We Detangle, But We Don't Explain

We work it out in the mirror.

Wide tooth. No tears. Soft hands-on stubborn strands We've carried for years.

We part what hurts.

Oil what stays.

Twist what's growing.

Clip what's in the way.

We don't beg you to get it.

We don't owe you the map. We been making miracles in silence and naps.

You see the curl.

You don't see the storm.

You see the style.

You missed the form.

So hush.

Respect the crown, not the pain. We detangle... but we don't explain.

He Loved Me Out Loud

He didn't whisper me.

He sang me.

In public, in group chats, in slow walks past strangers.

He didn't ask for quiet love— he brought the mic.

Told the world,

"That one? She mine. She magic."

He met me like Sunday.

Held me like breath. Let me be soft without asking what I cost.

It wasn't the flowers, it was the knowing. How he showed up like he had always known me.

He loved me out loud.

And now?

That's the only kind I hear.

We Had Great Chemistry, Bad Timing, and No Business

The spark?

Electric.

The glances?

Dangerous.

The way we laughed.

Should've been illegal.

But baby… we were two clocks set to different cities.

Always catching each other five minutes too late.

We had vibe.

But no vision.

We had heat.

But no shelter. We had hands, but didn't know what to hold.

Some loves burn.

Ours did. Beautiful, but not built to last.

And that's okay.

Some stories ain't meant for sequel. Just for spark, and a soft goodbye.

What I Learned from a Broken Heart

I learned that silence speaks. That loneliness has a sound.
That love can be loud even when it's not around.

I learned I can cry and keep moving.

Grieve and still glow.

That pain don't always mean stop— sometimes it means grow.

I learned to reread the signs.

To trust the no.

To stop watering gardens that don't want to really grow.

I learned my love is rich.

My peace is power. That healing ain't soft— it's a full-time hour.

And when I put the pieces down, I found something new:

I didn't lose me.

I just outgrew you.

Looking for a New Kind of Love

I'm not chasing butterflies.

I'm building gardens.

The love I want.

It grows.

It stays.

It guards me like armor.

I'm not looking for loud.

I've heard enough noise. I'm craving the kind that don't need to prove itself to feel real.

The kind that holds the door and the conversation.

That listens.

That learns.

That doesn't confuse silence with distance.

I want love that smells like peace. Feels like ease. Moves like, "I got you," without saying a word.

That’s what I’m looking for now— Not perfect.

But present.

Not wild.

But worth it.

Traveled Across the World, Only to Come Back to This

I sipped espresso in Italy.

Wrote poems in Spain. Danced with strangers who never asked me to dance.

I stood in rooms where no one knew my name— and somehow,

I felt more seen than I ever did at home.

I kissed under foreign moons, woke up to new songs, washed off years of pretending in the hotel sink.

And yet— I came back.

To familiar streets.

Familiar lips. Familiar lies.

You were still here.

Still wrong. Still hoping I'd forget everything I learned when I left.

I traveled across the world just to come back to this— and realize

I don't live here anymore.

Cakes, Pies, Cookies, and Weed

I don't need a man— I need a peach cobbler. A little lemon pound, and a hit from my mini-sized bubbler.

I've been ghosted, gaslit, grinding too long. So tonight, it's soft lights, warm sweets, and a chill song.

I've tried journaling.

Therapy.

Cardio.

Prayer.

But baby, sometimes

I just want butter and air.

A brownie for the pain. A blunt for the past. A cookie for the chaos that somehow didn't last.

So no, I'm not taking calls.

And no, I'm not out in these streets.

I'm home—full, high, healing on cakes, pies, cookies… and peace.

My Next Gig Will Be for Me

No more yes outta guilt.

No more "sure" through clenched teeth. No more glam for ghosts, no more smiling with grief.

I've shown up for stages that didn't know my worth. Painted faces while mine cracked in the mirror first.

I've worked for "exposure."

I've waited on "maybe."

But my talent ain't a favor.

And I'm done shrinking daily.

So my next gig?

It'll light me up.

Pay me fair.

Treat me kind.

And if it doesn't— I decline.

My next gig will match my value.

Will honor my name. Will pour into me what I've always gave.

My Makeup Brushes Tell a Story

Each bristle holds a whisper— a laugh from backstage, a tear on set, a secret from a face the world forgets.

This one took sweat off a news anchor five minutes before she told the nation we were at war. This one blended bruises on a singer who swore she "just fell."

This one? It touched cheeks that would never smile again.

And still… it dusts hope like glitter.

My brushes don't lie. They've seen nerves.

Seen power. They've shaped kings and queens and helped me hold myself together one swipe at a time.

These aren't just tools.

They're testimony.

My makeup brushes?

They tell my makeup story.

That Fur Coat with Nothing Underneath

It wasn't the fur.

It was the feeling. The hush of the room when I walked in, heat under velvet, confidence on skin.

No bra.

No backup.

No Plan B. Just me, and the hush I carried like perfume.

He looked.

They whispered.

But baby, I wasn't for sale. I was a warning in heels, wrapped in pleasure, and just outta reach.

Sometimes you wear lace.

Sometimes you wear armor.

But that night,

I wore the truth— soft, loud, and free.

That fur coat with nothing underneath wasn't about seduction.

It was about not hiding Not a damn thing.

Lipstick, Wine, and Late-Night Danger

It started with red.

On my lips.

On my glass. In the way I walked past without asking for permission.

It was one of those nights when the mirror said "go," and my soul said,

"Don't behave tonight."

I wasn't looking for trouble.

But I wasn't duckin' it either.

I knew my name.

He knew the risk.

The jazz played slow.

Our hearts didn't.

He asked what I wanted.

I said, "This moment."

He asked what I feared.

I said, "Waking up empty."

But baby, I didn't. I woke up full— of stories, of fire, of everything I used to hide.

Lipstick.

Wine.

And late-night danger. Sometimes the messiest nights are the ones that remind you you're alive.

I Overheard Your Ignorance and I Love It

You were loud.

Confident in your confusion. Dripping in wrong, but saying it like scripture.

And I?

I just sipped. Didn't flinch.

Didn't fix. Didn't offer my brilliance to your bargain-bin opinion.

Because there's power in letting folks be wrong. Letting them flex with no weight. Letting them speak and show their own lack.

I used to argue.

Used to correct.

Now?

I observe.

I collect the moment

like a little gift of delusion.

I overheard your ignorance— and baby,

I love it.

Because it reminds me exactly who not to be.

Money Money No Money

It's giving:

direct deposit— immediately gone. "Let's do brunch!"

Girl, I'm eating at home.

It's giving: credit score vibes.

"Pending payment" pride. Manifesting abundance with $4.75 inside.

One day I'm rich—

in plans, in hair, in glow.

Next day I'm googling

"Can you reuse foil tho?"

Money, money… no money. But somehow,

I stay funny.

Still show up.

Still shine. Still tipping God with what ain't mine.

So don't let the lashes fool you. The gloss, the 'gram, the flex. We budgeting like a prayer circle and lookin' good doing it, next.

A Hustler's Fatigue

I'm tired in the soul.

Not the eyes.

Not the back. But that place under my spirit where ambition use to clap.

I've shown up on E.

Poured from cracked cups.

Smiled while drowning.

Clapped while burning up.

Success don't taste sweet when you're always in motion. And dreams feel like deadlines when rest ain't the potion.

I've hustled for yes.

For checks.

For clout.

But now?

I just want to breathe without proving my route.

So today I rest.

Not because I'm lazy— but because I'm sacred. Because no grind is worth me losing that part of me.

The Side-By Affair

I wasn't your secret.

But I wasn't your claim. I was the comfort between chaos, the peace without a name.

You called me "magic."

You called me "safe."

But never "mine."

Never "stay."

I got the good mornings.

The deep talks.

The hands.

But not the plans.

Not the posts.

Not the ring.

We were...

right next to something real. So close I could feel it, but not close enough to hold.

You were loud in my silence.

Soft in my storms.

Present in my lonely.

Absent in my form.

And now I know— being almost loved is the most dangerous place to be.

I’ve Become Emotionally Unavailable

Not because I don’t feel— but because I feel too much. And too often, for people who felt me last.

I used to hand out pieces like party favors.

Now?

You get a nod.

A blink.

A boundary.

I still care.

But I don’t volunteer.

I don’t audition for intimacy. Don’t stretch for crumbs while calling it connection.

My softness is on lockdown.

Not gone—just gated. You can knock, but don’t expect keys if you ain’t sacred.

I’ve become emotionally unavailable.

And strangely? I’ve never felt more whole.

Lemon Drop Martinis and Truffle Fries

I took myself out tonight.

No table for two. Just me, the glow, and a little extra butter too.

Bartender smiled, called me "trouble in a glass." I sipped slow— let the citrus kissed my ass.

Truffle fries came hot.

The playlist knew me. I dipped every bite like I never had to share a damn thing.

No "what you doing?" texts.

No fake laughter. Just the kind of night you don't apologize for after.

A little lipstick.

A lot of vibes. Joy that don't need witness to feel alive.

So if you see me, smiling at nothing, lemon drop in hand— just know:

this is what healing tastes like.

Slipping Into My Darkness

I don't fight it anymore.

I let it wrap me.

Soft.

Heavy.

Honest.

There's no mask in the dark.

No need to smile. No need to fix what just needs to feel.

My shadow knows me.

She whispers truth when the light gets loud. She doesn't ask for pretty— just presence.

So I slip in. Not to break, but to breathe. Not to hide, but to heal.

Because sometimes the most sacred part of you is the one you buried deepest.

And tonight?

I dig with grace.

He Kissed My Toes Like A Pro

Didn't rush.

Didn't ask. Just lifted my foot like it was glass.

Laid a kiss like worship— slow, sweet, with heat in the hush.

You ever been adored from the ankle up? That "let me love the part most men skip" type touch?

He didn't moan.

He hummed.

Like he found gold in my arch. And baby—

I curled.

Not from fear,

but from art.

He kissed my toes like a pro.

Like a man who knows that pleasure starts at the first yes—and don't rush the rest.

Air Kiss Me in the Dark

You never touched me— not really.

But I still felt it.

In the way your silence brushed my name.

You spoke with eyes, but blinked too long. You reached— but only when I was already gone.

We had a rhythm,

but no sound. A flame, but no spark on the ground.

You air kissed me in the dark— and I called it love, because it floated like it meant to land.

But sweetheart ...

I need more than wind.

I need hands.

I need heat.

I need light that stays when morning comes back.

I Don't Chase Ghosts, I Name Them

I used to wonder why you disappeared.

Replay the silence.

Blame the echo.

Blame me.

But now? I call you what you are— unfinished. unavailable. unreal.

You ghosted, but left fingerprints.

And I collected them.

Turned them into poetry. Turned them into proof that I was always there.

You thought your exit would define me. But I'm still standing— whole, hooded, and holding your name like a lesson I finally passed.

I don't chase ghosts.

I name them. And then I keep walking—

light,

loud, and living.

His Energy

He walked in before his name did. And I felt it— thick, sweet, a little suspicious.

His energy wasn't loud, but it lingered. Like smoke with secrets. Like jazz in a room that used to be quiet.

He smiled.

But his vibe said

"Handle with care."

Said he'd been loved wrong.

And maybe did the same.

I listened. Not to his words, but to the way the room bent around him. The way my gut whispered "Maybe not." The way my peace paused.

His energy?

It wasn't bad.

But it wasn't mine. And that's enough to say goodbye without a reason.

Strength Comes in Numbers

One voice is brave.

Two is a threat.

Ten? That's a whole shift they can't forget.

We've held each other through breakups and breakthroughs, passed lashes and lessons like communion. Heard "you good?" and answered with

"Let's pour a drink."

We don't all speak the same— but we hum in harmony. We don't always agree— but we show up.

Because strength comes when the quiet ones nod. When the tired ones text.

When the strong ones say,

"Not today—rest."

You don't need the world when your girls got your back.

We are soft.

We are loud.

We are many.

And we're never going back.

My Sisterhood Is for My Sister Hood

We don't just match outfits— we match energy.

Hold space.

Hold hands.

Hold secrets that never made it to the group chat.

We show up with edge and earrings.

With Shea butter and shade. We bring greens, gospel, and "Girl, you better get up."

My sisterhood don't scream for applause.

We scream for each other. At jobs, at protests, at baby showers where the healing starts over cake.

This ain't that cute club.

This ain't filtered feminism.

This is:

"I'll walk with you through this mess."

"Here—take my charger."

"Text me when you make it home."

My sisterhood is for my sister hood.

From block to boardroom.

From press-on to PhD. We hold each other down— not just up.

Sometimes I Smell Like a French Whore, and I Loved It

I layered three perfumes.

Not by accident.

But because today

I wanted to smell like

pleasure and problems.

Like lipstick on napkins.

Like Chanel and secrets. Like don't ask me where I've been—
just be glad I came back.

You say, "too strong."

I say, "too unforgettable."

You say "too much."

I say "Exactly."

I walked past.

And your memory followed. Because I don't dab scent— I
announce it.

Sometimes I smell like a French whore.

And I loved it.

Because I deserve to enter a room like a feeling you can't scrub off.

His Strut Got Me Trippin'

He walked like he knew every eye was his.

Like the sidewalk owed him applause.

Like rhythm lived in his spine.

It wasn't the fit. (Though, Lord… the fit.) It was the tempo.

The "don't rush me" glide. The "you see me" smirk under his stride.

I tripped.

Not over my heels— but over the possibility.

Of conversation.

Of sin. Of just watching him leave and calling that a win.

His strut said,

"I've arrived."

And my soul said,

"Well damn, so have I."

His strut got me trippin'— but I ain't mad. Sometimes confidence

is the first thing I kiss before I even get his name.

1. He Was Fine but Exhausting
2. The Side Eye
3. I Protest, I Sit, I Wait… and the Same Sh*t
4. Voodoo Queen
5. People Stop Saying Thank You
6. No Ring? He's Married
7. If I Should Die Before I Drink
8. How Many Ways to Say Fuck Off
9. How to Say Fuck Off at Work
10. Instant Gratification
11. My Afro, My Rules
12. We Detangle, But We Don't Explain (centerpiece poem)
13. What I Learned from a Broken Heart
14. Looking for a New Kind of Love
15. Traveled Across the World, Only to Come Back to This
16. Cakes, Pies, Cookies, and Weed
17. My Next Gig Will Be for Me
18. My Makeup Brushes Tell a Story
19. That Fur Coat with Nothing Underneath
20. Lipstick, Wine, and Late-Night Danger
21. I Overheard Your Ignorance and I Love It
22. Money Money No Money
23. A Hustler's Fatigue
24. The Side-By Affair

25. I've Become Emotionally Unavailable
26. Lemon Drop Martinis and Truffle Fries
27. Slipping Into My Darkness
28. He Kissed My Toes Like A Pro
29. Air Kiss Me in the Dark
30. I Don't Chase Ghosts, I Name Them
31. His Energy
32. Strength Comes in Numbers
33. My Sisterhood Is for My Sister Hood
34. Sometimes I Smell Like a French Whore, and I Loved It
35. His Strut Got Me Trippin'
36. We Had Great Chemistry, Bad Timing, and No Business
37. Sis, I Ain't Sorry
38. His lips Smelled Like Doublemint Gum & Cigarettes
39. Emotionally Unavailable (visual created)
40. Fro Gurl's Recipe for Soft Recovery (Cakes, Pies, etc. visual)

Made in the USA
Columbia, SC
21 June 2025

59686768R00033